Martial Arts Philosophy and Wisdom

Proverbs, Sayings, and Quotes Used in Martial Arts

知

恵

Compiled and analyzed by
Kevin Dewayne Hughes

Ace Kiwami Publications

Pre-edition Copy Right 2013 (100 made) under the title:
Warrior Wisdom: Proverbs, Sayings, and Quotes Used in Martial Arts

Martial Arts Philosophy and Wisdom: Proverbs, Sayings, and Quotes Used in Martial Arts

Author: Kevin Dewayne Hughes

1st edition Copy Right 2013
2nd edition Copy Right 2022

The information in this book is for informational purposes only. The publishers, authors, producers, associates, affiliates, and those involved in the production of this work are not and will not be held responsible, in any way whatsoever, for any use made by anyone of the information contained in this book. All use of the information in this book must be made in accordance with what is permissible by law, and any damage liable to be caused as a result thereof will be the exclusive responsibility of the user. This book is intended to be used in conjunction with ongoing training taught by an authorized expert in the field. This book is not a substitute for formal training. It is the sole responsibility of the user to consult with a licensed physician in order to obtain complete medical information on the user's ability and limitations. It is also the user's responsibility to inform the expert instructor(s) of these abilities and limitations. This book is in no way to be used as a substitute for medical treatment or for medical, emotional, or mental counseling with a licensed physician, psychiatrist, psychologist, councilor, or other healthcare provider.

2

Dedication
This book as well as the previous edition is dedicated to my daughters Samantha and Isabel. They are the reasons I write so they can have record of their legacy.

This edition is also dedicated to my son Kayden.

Preface to the 1ˢᵗ edition

Over the years, I have heard many words of wisdom concerning the way of the martial arts. I have compiled many of these saying in this book.

I have noticed that some quotes have been erroneously contributed to one person when in fact another person said it. Sometimes, a master would quote another master from the past in their writings without giving recognition. This would lead to the quote being passed down as if the master were the originator of the quote. Now I have done by best to ensure that the quotes are attributed to the correct person. However, future research may reveal more information that will lead to revisions in future editions of this text.

Some of these sayings originate out of certain Eastern religions and influence martial arts philosophy. Read these as simple words of wisdom and try to understand them. Do not worry if it comes from a religion not your own. The only point here is to understand the martial philosophy of past warriors who had to rely on their martial arts because it was a matter of life and death.

I am a Christian and I have found that I can read the quotes that originate out of another religion without it influencing my relationship with Jesus. As such, I have included in an appendix, Biblical references concerning the ways of the warrior.

Kevin Dewayne Hughes
27 February 2013

Preface to the 2nd Edition

Instead of the second edition being a restatement of quotes in the first edition, I have decided to expand each quote with my thoughts and ideas conjured by the quote. This is why the first edition was one book and the second edition is expanded into volumes. The appendices of the first book will be placed into its own volume in the second edition.

Please be sure to read the thoughts and think about them. See if you agree or disagree with my thoughts and then justify why you agree or disagree. Reflect and grow.

With the first edition, I asked my students to think about the quotes and see what thoughts and ideas they had. In the second edition, I am doing what I asked my students to do with the first edition.

Kevin Dewayne Hughes
29 June 2020

Working 10 to 12 hour days six days a week delayed the final completion of this text.

Table of Contents

Bonus Chapter: On Bunkai
Find this in the hardcover edition

Introduction

In the past, the warrior met the enemy toe-to-toe. It was not uncommon for the warrior to not only see the face of the enemy, but to know the enemy's emotions during engagement. Today, most warriors never have such experience as the enemy is usually down range of the rifle. With drone warfare, the impersonalization of the enemy is even more pronounced.

Not only did the warrior of the past have different battlefield experiences than the soldiers of today, but matters of self-defense and self-protection were also different. It was more common for the martial artist of the past to engage in some form of self-defense action than it is for the modern martial artist. Therefore, the sayings of past warriors give the modern martial artist insight into the thinking and philosophy of those who had to use their martial arts for life and death.

Not only are the sayings of past warriors important, but also the saying of philosophers and religions are important to the warrior. The reason is that these philosophers and religions influenced the course of the martial arts philosophy and thinking. When reading these quotes, try to step into the mind, time period, and location of the person to help understand the essence of the quote.

Philosophy and Wisdom

Sun Tzu

To subdue the enemy without fighting is the highest skill.

Thoughts

War is not pretty. There is no glory in killing other people or things for no reason. It is usually the governments ... the politicians ... the elitists that are at war. The soldier and the enemy soldier both have lives, families, and loved ones. They are only fighting because the powers that be told them too.

Rarely is war such that the enemy soldiers all deserve death and destruction. Do not get me wrong. There are such evils in the world that do deserve total annihilation of the entire enemy such as the Nazis of the Second Great War.

If victory can be achieved without death and destruction, then everyone on both sides will be better off. After all, the enemy warrior is your brother in arms. He just fights on the other side. Being brothers in arms also means one should hope to have similar treatment from the enemy, which if honor is to be had, it will be given.

The Author with his Filipino student Eman Monteclaro.

Morihei Ueshiba
Ultimately, you must forget about technique. The further you progress, the fewer teachings there are. The Great Path is really NO PATH.

Thoughts
In the beginning of martial arts training, a student sees many, many different styles. There are boxing styles, wrestling styles, weapons styles, internal styles, soft styles, hard styles, external styles, etc. It can be overwhelming.

However, the old martial arts of the deep past were comprehensive. They just started in different places for their training. Eventually, a martial artist that studied long enough would start to see less and less differences in the martial arts and realize that ultimately there is only one style of martial art and that is the human style. As time progressed further, the martial artist realized that all the techniques learned reduces to a small handful of techniques that the specific individual uses in real situations. As the old idea goes: One comes full circle and ends where they began.

Shinkage-ryu Kenjutsu (unknown)
Victory goes to the one who has no thought
of himself.

Thoughts
Being worried for yourself. Being worried
that you will be hurt. Being worried that you
will loose. Being worried that you will die.
All these thing preoccupy the mind.

Do not worry. Do not think. Just be and let
your training be your action.

A distracted mind leads to defeat.

The author with a student, Buddy Wolfe in the mid 1990s.

Lao Tzu

He who defends with love will be secure;
Heaven will save him, and protect him with
love.

Thoughts

Now the base of this is iffy.

However, the underlying premise is sound:
act out of love not hate.

Even if Heaven and love does not save the
warrior and the warrior pays the ultimate
sacrifice, the warrior will be favorably
remembered if actions were taken out of
love.

Although not stated in the quote, the idea is
to fight out of love of family, friends, and
countrymen. If one fights out of hate like the
Nazis did, then the an overwhelming force of
good will rise up to defeat them. So in this
regard, maybe Heaven and love could be
seen as the savior of the warrior who fights
evil.

Tsunetomo Yamamoto
Tether even a roasted chicken.

Thoughts
This seems to be an odd warrior quote.
However, it is very important to heed its
advice. What this is saying, is that even when
the enemy is so thoroughly defeated that
there is nothing more they can do, keep your
guard up because they may have a surprise in
store for you.

Kata teach this as a very important concept in
the use of zanshin. Zanshin is the remaining
mind or continual mind. I have seen it being
taught with two purposes. One is to keep
being aware of what is around you for
another attacker or the defeated attacker to
attack again. The other purpose is to savor
the victory. Too not drop the mental attitude
of being engaged in the fight even after the
fight has ended.

I learned this lesson well in one my school
yard fights when I was in elementary school
in Germany. I had knocked a bully down to
the ground and pinned him there. He could
not get up. He apologized and asked me to

let him up. I complied and as he was standing he sucker punched me and the fight ensued again.

From that lesson I learned to never let anyone up after subduing them. If I subdue someone, I tell them not to move as I release them and I further tell them if the so much as twitch I will begin kicking them in the ribs or some other target. I tell them to not move until I say they can, and I make sure I am at a safe distance and they have no weapons on them that they can use on me once they get back to their feet.

Lord Shang

When people are stupid, they think force easy but cleverness difficult. But if the world is clever, then it finds knowledge easy but force difficult.

Thoughts

This is saying that stupid people resort to violence to solve problems because they are too stupid to come up with a non-violent solution. However, those that are intelligent enough to come up with a non-violent solution are usually poorly skilled in violence.

The idea is balance. The warrior should be skilled in violence but should also be trained in the ways of the mind so that they can discern the most peaceful solution to a problem but still be able to use violence if needed.

Sun Tzu
Victory is reserved for those who are willing to pay its price.

Thoughts
Victory can be costly in spent lives, spent equipment, and spent supplies. In some cases victory can be achieved where the enemy pays more than the victor. However, in some cases, the victor must pay more than the enemy.

When I was in the U.S. Army, one of my commanding officers told me that the hardest part of his job was deciding who should die. Sometimes victory is secured by sending a small force to distract the enemy knowing that the small force will be all killed. Unfortunately, victory would not have been had, if this small force was not sacrificed.

The author doing Yoga

Isshin-ryu Karate (Unknown)
The time to strike is when the opportunity presents itself.

Thoughts
The questions are: How to define the opportunity? Can we create the opportunity?

Yes, we can create the opportunity. For example, a distraction can create an opportunity. Unfortunately a discussion of creating opportunity is beyond the scope of this text.

So what is an opportunity? It is a moment of weakness or exposure in the enemy that can be exploited. A complete discussion of this is also beyond the scope of this text.

Lao Tzu

When the people of the world all know beauty as beauty, there arises the recognition of ugliness. When they all know good as good, there arises the recognition of evil.

Thoughts

The definition of good relies on evil to be defined just as the definition of evil relies on good to be defined. What is evil to one society may not be evil to another just as what is good to one society may not be good to another.

Fortunately, there are universal standards. For example: murder is wrong. However, in other issues, the definitions of right and wrong, good and evil, or beauty and ugly, are not set to a universal standard. Therefore, be educated on other societies so that you can understand those differences and act appropriately.

Chotoku Kyan
A punch should stay like a treasure in the
sleeve. It should not be used
indiscriminately.

Thoughts
Be capable of violence but do not use it
unless it is absolutely necessary. If you are
not capable of violence then you will fail if
you ever need to be violent. Times when
violence is absolutely necessary include
defense of life and the things that make life
possible.

A distinction should be drawn between
violence using raw savagery and viciousness,
and the violence seen in a gentlemanly bout.

Lao Tzu

Those who know don't talk. Those who talk don't know.

Thoughts

Like I have been known to say: "The bigger the mouth the smaller the fight." In other words, the more knowledgeable, confident, and skilled a person is, the less they need to talk. Whereas, the less knowledgeable, confident, and skilled a person is, they tend to compensate by running their mouth about the subject or attempt to showoff what little they know. Showing off what little they know is like wrapping a roll of one dollar bills with a one hundred dollar bill on the outside to create the illusion that they are richer than they are.

If you are confident in your knowledge and ability, there is no need to brag, talk, or show off. Others will brag and talk about you and your reputation will precede you.

Sun Tzu
The dance of battle is always played to the same impatient rhythm. What begins in a surge of violent motion is always reduced to the perfectly still.

Thoughts
This appears to deal with large scale combat in that everything happens fast and things slow as the soldiers fatigue and die.

However, does the same apply to individual combat? An individual will follow the same general high energy and slow as fatigue sets in. This spells out a strategy for both large and small scale combat. Make the enemy become fatigued before you and then destroy them.

Fatigue is more than just physical exhaustion. It also can be mental exhaustion and spiritual exhaustion.

When I was in the U.S. Army I was taught that the enemy goes for these three targets: 1) Communications such as the radio guy or communications equipment. 2) Heavy guns such as M-60s and 50 caliber machine guns.

3) Chaplain, chaplain assistant and other religious items. The idea is cause mental and spiritual fatigue before causing total physical fatigue and defeat. This is the essence to what I have said before: "I destroy minds and spirits before destroying the physical body."

I was also taught in the U.S. Army that a terrorist attack on a US military installation targets these three things in this order. 1) Officers to cut the head off the chicken or snake. 2) Equipment to reduce ability and readiness. 3) Chaplain and chaplain assistant to say their god is superior.

Dan Baughman one of the author's best friends and yudansha student of the Tenkidokan.

Miyamoto Mushashi

The sword has to be more than a simple weapon; it has to be an answer to life's questions.

Thoughts

The sword has long been seen as a gentleman's weapon. In this regard the sword is more than a simple weapon. It is a weapon of class and character. Swords are often named and some believed to be imbued with magical powers.

A sword is also a tool of peace and a tool of war. As a tool of war, it is a simple weapon. As a tool of peace, it keeps the peace by holding would be invaders at bay. Similar to how a lock on a box is there to keep an honest person honest.

The second statement about being an answer to life's questions tends to apply to all martial arts. This is one thing that differentiates a martial art from a fighting system. All real martial arts contain a fighting system or a complement to a fighting system. But they are so much more in that they develop the body, mind, and spirit to higher levels than a

mundane existence alone would allow.
Where as a fighting system only develops
fighting skill, a real martial art develops
fighting skills and many other things. In this
way, the sword has become an answer to
life's questions.

The Author with Ben Smith and Ron Shively

Bokuden Tsukahara
Mental bearing, not skill, is the sign of a
matured samurai.

Thoughts
Physical skill can be developed at a young
age. But a warrior is developing more than
just physical skill. The mind and the spirit of
a warrior are also developed.

The brain is thought to continue physical
development until the mid twenties. While
the brain goes through physical changes,
there are resulting mental changes. Even
after physical development of the brain is
complete, the brain continues development
with chemical changes as the brain ages.

The whole purpose of life is spiritual growth
and development since our bodies are just
the caterpillar stage for our spirits to become
the matured butterflies in the next life.

Courage, fear, and all emotions stem from
the spirit in the three-body view of our
existence. Without the spirit, the brain
would just be a computer doing whatever the
internal and external stimuli tell that

computer to do and that would be things in accordance to its programming.

Therefore, a warrior skilled in physical techniques but too afraid to apply them is worthless as a warrior. Mental bearing and spiritual development are also needed to ensure a warrior does not take irrational actions or act to hastily and cause unjustified harm when a more peaceful solution could have been found.

The Author with Jake Lahniers, one of this best friends and top student at the Tenkidokan.

31

Bruce Lee

Empty your mind. Be formless, shapeless, like water. Now put water into a cup, it becomes the cup. You put water into a bottle; it becomes the bottle. You put water into a teapot; it becomes the teapot. Now water can flow, or it can crash. Be water my friends.

Thoughts

The alchemical elements are more like states of matter than they are like chemical elements. The classic Greek alchemical elements are: air, fire, water, and earth. In Eastern thought everything is divided into fives. The Chinese have five elements that are usually listed as: fire, metal, wood, earth, and water. However, this is not the only Chinese five-element system. Instead of listing another Chinese five-element system, I will list the Japanese version of the five elements: fire, earth, water, sky (air), void (nothingness or empty space).

Water has some amazing properties like Bruce Lee pointed out. However, it is important to be able to move between the properties of the elements. There is a time to be crash like water, but there is a time to burn like fire. There is a time to be steady like rock, but a time to be untouchable like air.

Water cannot burn but fire can. Water cannot root, but wood can. Water cannot resist, but earth can.

Learn to change with the times and the situation, which that too will change and evolve as time flows, so that you can set yourself up to be at the best advantage in life.

Do not restrict yourself to understanding just one element system. Learn them all and their characteristics. This will help in deciphering ancient martial methods.

The Author's wife

Bokuden Tsukahara

A samurai, therefore, should neither be pompous nor arrogant.

Thoughts

This is something I see often out of the sports crowd where name-calling and insults are used to entertain the crowd and then leads to poor behavior by players outside the competition. It is one thing to use taunts while engaged in conflict in an attempt to enrage the opponent into making a mistake. However, the distasteful display of barbarism and calling it martial arts is poor game by anyone that does anything called martial arts.

Pompous, elitist, arrogant, holier than though attitudes should not be the behavior of the warrior. The warrior is the servant of others. It is the warrior who sometimes choses to lay down their life in the protection of the lives of the non-warrior. In this role of servitude, the warrior has no room to think that they are better than others.

Lao Tzu
An over sharpened sword cannot last long.

Thoughts
This is true of most things a nature. An overly bright and massive star burns out faster than the smaller, dimmer ones.

This even applies to our bodies in martial arts training. Being too hard will burn the body out sooner and the life will not be as long. The body will break sooner as well.

In the case of an art like Tai Chi Chuan, the sword is not very sharp but the sword last a very long time. In an art like Karate, the sword is very sharp but the sword breaks down more quickly. In time, an art like Tai Chi Chuan must become more hard while an art like Karate must become more soft as the student develops. In the end, the two should come to a common point so that both are of equal sharpness. The two become a mix of hard and soft.

Just as a note: Sparring is considered sharpening the sword. Tai Chi Chuan practitioners must spar to sharpen that sword for combat. Push-hands does not cut it as it is not sparing. Rather, push-hands is a tool for training.

Another note: I always tell my students train a soft internal art and a hard external art together for maximum benefit. Though it is their choice.

Lieh Tzu

No man will confide in one who shows himself as aggressive. And he whom no man will confide in will remain solitary and without support.

Thoughts

I wish this were absolutely true. Unfortunately, pricks tend to congregate together. Therefore, pricks (aggressive people) will not live a solitary life. The part that is true is that they will not have real support. Any support they think they have will be false and easily torn from underneath them.

By being mild mannered and only aggressive when needed, you will attract more people like yourself and have a life with less stress. Unfortunately, the support being genuine is going to be based on the heart of the people you surround yourself with and this could also be false support.

Kenwa Mabuni
Karate is a lifetime study.

Thoughts
All martial arts are a lifetime study. There is always something new about a movement that can be learned. This is especially true when considering that the mind and body change as we age. How a movement worked when we were younger will not be executed the same when we are older.

This is one purpose of bunkai or the analysis of the kata movements. It is to ensure that the techniques work for the practitioner's mind and body and that moment. Considering this purpose, bunkai is never done. It is a task that must be done often throughout one's life to ensure the movements will work in an emergency situation of sudden onslaught aggression. Even things as simple as ippon kumite must go through bunkai to ensure proper function for a real situation.

Lao Tzu
He who strikes with a sharp point will not himself be safe for long.

Thoughts
This is basically saying that those who live by the sword will die by the sword. If you go looking for trouble, you will find it.

The goal of martial arts is to live as long as possible; to not die. If you go around being overly aggressive, you will eventually find yourself in a situation where you match up against a superior opponent or those whom you made angry will lay a trap for you.

Be respectful and kind to everyone to help ensure as long a life as possible. Being a generally good person will also help others to want to return respect and kindness to you.

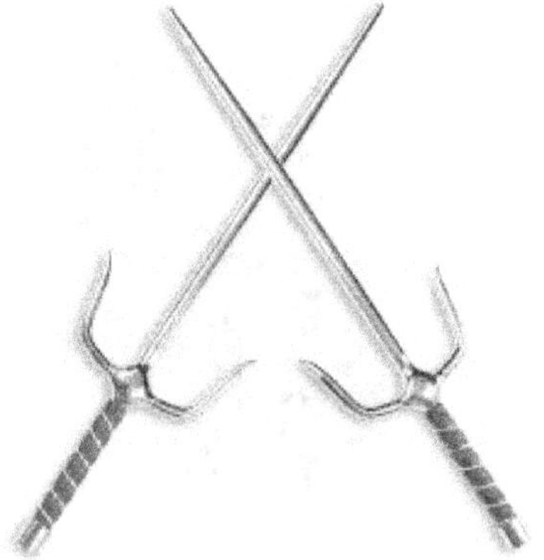

Miyamoto Musashi

There is nothing outside of yourself that can ever enable you to get better, stronger, richer, quicker, or smarter. Everything is within. Everything exists. Seek nothing outside of yourself.

Thoughts

The drive to do these things definitely comes from within. Unfortunately, there are outside forces that can affect motivation. There are also access issues. One cannot get smarter in a subject if they lack access to the information to learn the subject.

However, removing access issues and learning to ignore negative external forces will allow all to come from within.

Do not limit yourself.

Chinese Proverb
The superior man moves his lips. The common man moves his fists.

Thoughts
Fighting does not take much intelligence. In fact, it is a basic survival skill that most all living animals have except for humans. In fact, fighting is easy. All it is, is moving with the right timing to hurt, disable, or kill you're your opponent.

Technology and relative safety have made humans weak and depleted of viciousness. This was not always the case. In the not so distant past, weak humans died. Today, technology, modern medicine, and relative safety help the weak to thrive.

What sets humans apart from the other animals is the large capacity for intelligence. Someone that resorts to violence to solve problems is on the same level as all the other animals. However, the one that can be diplomatic with words is not only above the other animals but also above the other humans who think violence is the ultimate path.

This does not mean that fighting skills are useless to the superior man. On the contrary, the superior man must have fighting skills for when diplomacy fails or is not possible.

Kim Delauter, one of the Author's students and friends.

Guang Ping Yang Cheng Fu
The energy of the sword is like a rainbow;
The moving of the sword is like a dragon;
The sword and the spirit are fused into one;
The application of sword skill is magnificent.

Thoughts
Note that this is a poem about Wudang
swordsmanship.

Watching the master swordsman or any
master martial artist is beautiful and awe
inspiring. Martial arts bring beauty to death.
Not to death itself of the opponent, but to
the one dealing the death.

Oscar Mampa, one of the Author's students and friend.

Lao Tzu
Just remain in the center; watching, and then forget you are there.

Thoughts
In the grand scheme of the universe, each person is at the center since the universe has infinite volume. So realize you are always at the center of the universe.

In anything else, being in the center is usually the safest place. Take a herd of sheep for example. The sheep on the edge of the herd are in greater danger to become prey than the ones in the middle.

However, this has a deeper spiritual meaning. When I teach energy arts like Yoga and Qi Gong, I close with a guided meditation. During this guided meditation, the students are asked to bring their emotions to neutral and their thoughts to center. To center themselves and remain there while the guided meditation takes place. At center, everything is in balance and it is here that everything can reset and then grow evenly/symmetrically.

Unknown

A good fighter flees from the moment's danger.

Thoughts

A moment's danger could be each attack by the opponent. Avoid being hit by getting out of the way. One is not fleeing the opponent in this case. Rather, one is fleeing the danger of each individual attack.

This can also mean to only fight those fights that you know you can win and flee from all the fights you cannot win. Even Miyamoto Musashi, who was a renowned swordsman, would flee from a fight if he thought he could not win it. Unfortunately, there are times to engage in battles that you know you cannot win, such as sacrificing your life to save your loved one's life.

The Great Learning (Unknown)
What is truly within will be manifest on the outside.

Thoughts
People can try to hide who they are. Most people can keep their fake persona up for only a short time. Eventually, who they are will show. At first, it will be little bits here and there and then eventually the full real persona will emerge.

This means, that in order to become what you want to be, change must happen inside first. If you want to be the warrior, then you must become the warrior inside so that the warrior will manifest on the outside.

Additionally, a person's character cannot be known from one encounter. Do not be too hasty in making friends or falling in love. Given time, the true person will emerge and you might find that they are not a suitable friend or love.

Confucius
The superior man is distressed by his want of ability; he is not distressed by men not knowing him.

Thoughts
If the goal is to become recognized and famous, you will probably fail. Not always. But most often you will fail.

On the other hand, if you goal to become as best as you can at something, then fame will follow, as your reputation will precede you. That is, if you allow your skills and knowledge to be demonstrated in view of the public eye. However, if you keep your skills and knowledge private, no one will know you for that knowledge and skill set.

The goal should always be to grow and increase in skill and knowledge. Therefore, if one wants to be skilled and knowledgeable but keep it private, then this is a worthy goal. Fame is not for everyone and definitely should not be the goal.

She King
Be not like those ruled by their passions and desires.

Thoughts
Being dedicated to a passion or dedicated to achieving a desire is not the same as being ruled by it.

I desire my wife and this is a good thing for a successful marriage. However, I do not let my desire for my wife rule over me.

Martial arts is one of those things that one could easily let rule them. Being dedicated and passionate about learning martial arts is a good thing. Being ruled by martial arts is a bad thing.

The one ruled by martial arts will prioritize training over everything to the point of missing critical life events. The one who is dedicated and passionate about martial are but not ruled by martial arts will forgo a day of training to attend their child's special event.

Chuang Tzu
When men do not forget what should be easily forgotten, and forget what is not easily forgotten ... we have a case of real oblivion.

Thoughts
What should be easily forgotten? Petty sins are one thing. Holding a useless grudge only deepens hurt and divide and leads to time wasted in the grudge that could have gone to betterment of yourself.

What is something that should not be easily forgotten? Manners are one thing. Being polite and respectful is an easy thing to do. Lacking politeness and respect can lead to issues and problems that would never have manifested if good manners were used.

The Author's wife

Sun Tzu
To win one hundred victories in one hundred battles is not the highest skill.

Thoughts
Open warfare is always an option for dealing with an opponent, but it is the worst option. Physical warfare, economic warfare, psychological warfare, all forms of warfare should be avoided if it can be avoided. Even if you can decimate the enemy, open warfare should be the last resort. Warfare not only harms lives and the lives of those not involved in the conflict, but it destroys livelihood via property, environment, and economic damage.

An already enraged enemy will take more skill to calm and bring to negotiations than it takes to engage them into open warfare. Therefore, the more peaceful the victory, the higher the skill needed.

Morihei Ueshiba

In true budo there is no enemy or opponent. True budo is to become one with the universe, not train to become more powerful or to throw down some opponent. Rather we train in hopes of being of some use, however small our role may be, in the task of bringing peace to mankind around the world.

Thoughts

There is a distinct difference between budo and bujutsu and Morihei Ueshiba is telling us this difference. Budo is for betterment of oneself and the betterment of the world. The ability to engage another in combat has nothing to do with budo. Bujutsu, on the other hand, is about the ability to engage in combat.

Now a budoka (ka indicates a person who does the practice of) can become competent in combat if they adjust to train for combat. However, their focus is self development and world improvement.

A bujutsuka can improve self and the world by fighting to end conflicts so that peace is achieved and then maintained. Regardless, the focus of the bujutsuka is fight, subdue, maim, and kill.

This is why the martial arts I teach are both budo and bujutsu. My martial arts are trained for effectiveness in combat and this is the bujutsu part. However, I mentor and guide my students to become better more positive versions of themselves and I instill in them the desire and yearning to make the world a better place. This is the budo part.

A good read. Find it from many book sellers

Bruce Lee
Using no way as way.

Thoughts
There is always the Tao or Do in Japanese.
No matter what it is, there is some path that
one follows. When the path is the same as
others, then you become predictable by
others. By having no path as the path, then
you become a lot harder for people to predict
you.

By cutting your own path, you might make
new discoveries that others have not. You
might even rediscover something that has
been forgotten.

Walking a path that is not your normal path
but is a common path for others can allow
you to see things that those who normally
walk that path do not see because they have
become complacent on that path.

I use this in my scientific journey. I was a
hydrogeologist working as a filtration
engineer in charge of research and
development at a small company. Diesel
exhaust fluid (DEF) was close to being

required by law and we had to come up with a way to filter the fluid.

Diesel exhaust fluid is just urea at a specific purity and concentration. The urea would break down the filter material and make filtration impossible.

What I did, was use my medical background and realized that urine is filtered in medical labs for analysis. I found out what is used to filter urine and from that I developed the world's first viable diesel exhaust fluid filter.

Johnlester Amador, one of the Author's students and friends.

Lao Tzu
Knowing how to yield is strength.

Thoughts
Yielding can be a very powerful technique. Tai Chi Chuan is focused on yielding and then returning. Yielding to a force can allow you to join that force and multiply it like Aikijujutsu. A trap for an enemy can be sprung by yielding to their advance. So many ways that yielding can by used to one's advantage.

In addition, knowing when to take a loss or yielding requires strength. Sometimes, yielding and allowing the opponent to have something will result in a better outcome. There are times to just let someone have the victory in an argument if the subject is meaningless and/or harmless. Knowing when to give takes not only strength, but also courage.

This quote brings to mind another important point. In the dual existence of Yin and Yang, Yin is seen as weak while Yang is seen as strong. Yang gives while Yin receives. Yang is aggressive while Yin is passive. In almost all regards, it is Yang that is seen as the active powerhouse and Yin is seen as a do nothing weakness. However, Yin is just as powerful as Yang and the two are even more powerful together if they are used correctly together.

For example, yang can be push while yin is pull. If you push someone, you knock them back. Pulling them essentially knocks them forward. Here, it should be easy to see that Yin and Yang can both be equally powerful. Used in tandem, the act of pulling and pushing together does much more damage to the opponent than either one alone does.

In arts like karate, Yin and Yang is constant in the techniques. When doing a karate punch, the punching hand is the Yang hand while the hand going to chamber is the Yin hand. If the chambering hand is pulling a body part in while the punching hand is hitting the body then the force delivered into the opponent is much greater than what the punch alone would have delivered.

If you are unaware, the chambering hand in Karate is called hikite in Japanese. Hikite means the pulling hand or drawing hand as in drawing a drawer open. Chamber hand is meant to represent the action of pulling something in.

The Author's daughter doing one of her passions.

Bruce Lee
Having no limitation as limitation

Thoughts
All humans have limitations. However, no one is able to achieve their limits in a lifetime. There is always more to improve and grow to the day a person dies. Never stop growing and developing. Even when the improvement is minor, keep improving.

The Author

The Author and his wife

Shoshin Nagamine

Karatedo may be referred to as the conflict within yourself, or a life-long marathon, which can be won only through self-discipline, hard training, and your own creative efforts.

Thoughts

Here, Shoshin Nagamine describes Karate as a Budo. The conflict within describes yourself as the enemy of that conflict. In Budo, the enemy is yourself. In Bujutsu, the enemy is other people. In my martial arts, the enemy is the constant fight to kill your old self so that a newer, better version of you emerges from the ashes. This is the Budo part. In the Bujutsu part, the goal is learn violence to be able to stop and control the violence of evil people.

Both Budo and Bujutsu require hard training and self-discipline. Well, except Budo as recreation. Budoka who train for recreation do not require hard training.

What is interesting here is that Nagamine says that your own creative efforts are important. Does this mean alter the kata with creativity? Well, in Budo, this can very well be the case since the objective is not to train fight but to improve self. In Budo, feel free to alter the forms for your own personal flavor and expression. However, retain the template that you learned from for uniformity across an organization and/or style.

In Bujutsu, creativity is still needed. In the process of bunkai, which is a method to analyze the motion of the forms, creativity is needed to bunkai as well as to derive henka, or variations to the applications. Henka are important because there are too many situations and variables to train every single situation that could occur. Being able to derive Henka requires a creative mind to derive appropriate scenarios. Training can then be tailored to the specific scenarios one might encounter, which can be different by student and location.

Lao Tzu
Knowing others is intelligence; knowing yourself is wisdom.

Thoughts
I would add: What good is it to know others, if you do not know yourself.

Psychologists say that there are four views of an individual. 1) What I know about myself that others do not know. 2) What others know about me, that I do not know about myself. 3) What others and I know about me/myself. 4) Those things that neither others nor I know about me/myself.

This means that I can know about others to a degree, but what is the point if there are things about myself that I do not know. I should study myself to discover those things hidden from me about myself. By discovering the hidden things about myself, I can then reduce the weaknesses and deficiencies as well as enhance strengths I would not have understood otherwise.

The same knowing goes for others. By studying others you can find those hidden traits that can make them a friend or foe, to be kept or discarded, and any other category a person may need to be placed into.

The Author from his Army days

Chen Chiju

In war, always think of how to save lives.

Thoughts

War is not filled with glory like some think.
There is no honor in killing. The honor comes
in sparing life and the glory comes in saving
lives.

Unfortunately, to save lives might mean
taking lives. When forced into this be sure
that the number of lives saved is greater than
the number of lives taken. Do not look only
at the current situation but look at the whole
outcome.

If one were to have an encounter with a
murder who will murder one person per
week for ten years after running into them,
then that murder will kill a total of five
hundred and twenty people. By killing them,
the lives of five hundred and twenty people
have been saved. Now do not take this as
literal advice for the modern world. Please
allow the justice system to do its work and
remove the murder from the streets. Do not
take justice into your own hands.

I also am reminded of Batman saying that if you kill a killer that the number of killers in the world remains the same. Well ... if you kill lots of killers the number of killers in the world drops. Only look at the thinking. Do not become a vigilante and take justice into your own hands.

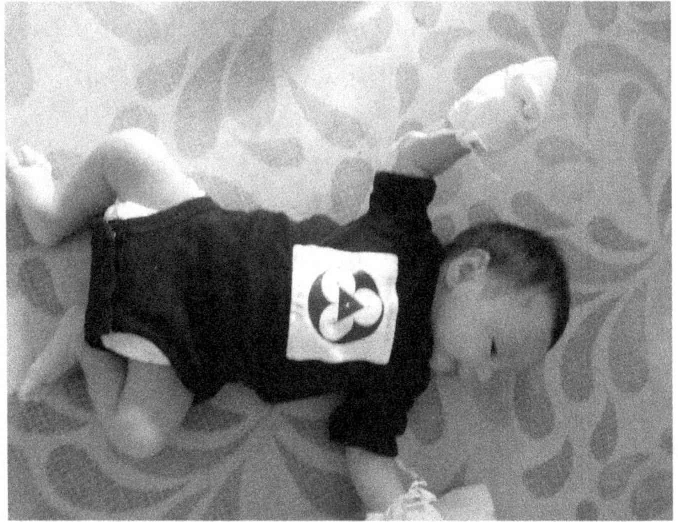

The Author's son ready to begin training.

Lao Tzu
Mastering others is strength; mastering yourself is true power.

Thoughts
Being able to dominate others is one thing. However, being reckless and haphazardous reduces one's abilities. Therefore mastering one's self leads to greater mastery of others.

Do not abuse any mastery over others. If others grant you mastery over them, then respect that position and lead them along the path they have asked you to lead them. If they work for you, treat them as your equal and pay them a fair wage.

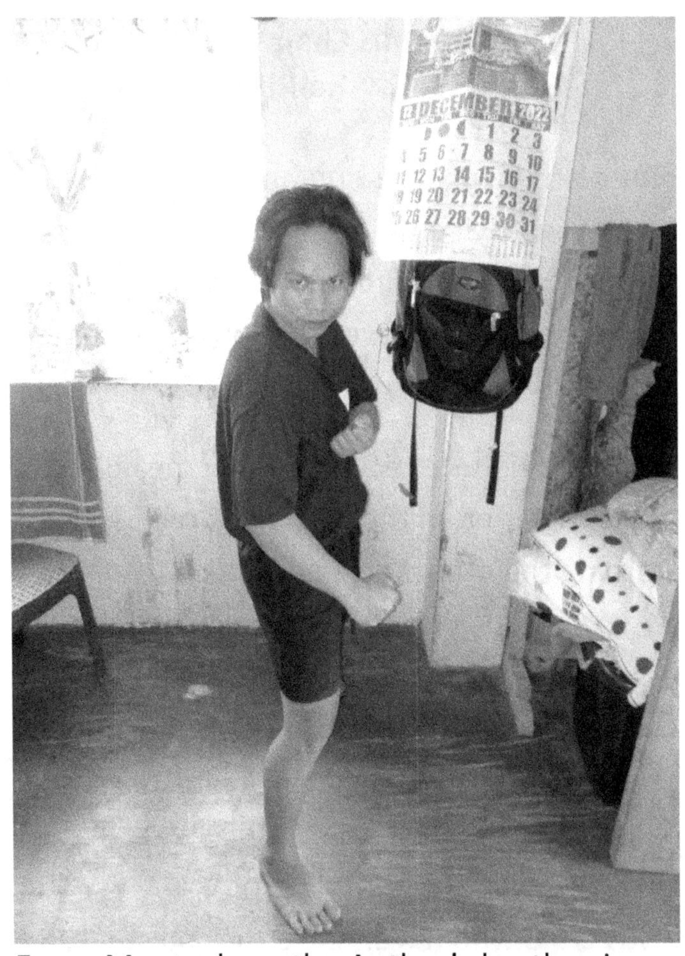

Eman Monteclaro, the Author's brother-in-law, top student in the Philippines, and friend. His nicknames include "Ip Eman" and "He-Eman."

Bonus Chapter
Shu-Ha-Ri

Shu-ha-ri is a progression one goes through as they learn and then grow in their training. The concept is not limited to martial arts but applies to any endeavor that one engages in that leads to personal growth.

Shu is the first stage and roughly means to come together. In the shu stage, one is learning their teacher's martial art. It is largely a game of mimicry. Those organizations that require everyone to do everything exactly the same limit the growth of students and the limit the ability of their students to grow out of the shu stage. In the long run, such schools will produce instructors who never leave the shu stage. Each passing generation will result in the degradation of the martial art until it becomes nothing more than a formal dance. Therefore, it is important to help your students and yourself to grow out of the shu stage.

Ha is the second stage and means to break. Some say it means to break away from your teacher. This is not the case. It means to break out of your teacher's mold and become your own. At this stage the student is no longer doing their teacher's martial art, but is now doing their own martial art. The teacher does the martial art as it works for the teacher and this may not work perfectly for the student. At the ha stage, the student is making the martial art work for them. This is why stagnation and degradation occur if all students are forced to remain in the shu stage.

Ri is the third and final stage and means to transcend. In this stage the student and the martial art have become one. Techniques flow as if it is their nature. Their state of mind has changed. In the shu and ha stages, the mind must tell the body to execute a technique. In the ri stage, the mind must tell the body not to execute a technique. What this means is that in the chaos of combat all their training just flows as if a dam holding back water was suddenly opened.

There is a saying out of Kyujutsu the art of samurai archery. They say that when an archer dies, the archer fires one last arrow. This is the embodiment of ri. The old archer is so accustomed to firing arrows that it has become the archer's nature. When the archer dies, and the mind releases control of the body, the body uses its remaining energy to fire another arrow because that is the nature of the archer.

The natural person must put in effort to fire the arrow while the transcended master must put in the effort to not fire the arrow.

Another way to look as shu-ha-ri is in the typicall parenting roles. The child is in the shu stage and mimics their parents while their parents mold them after themselves. When the child becomes an adult, life forces them to become their own person and they are now in the ha stage. When they raise their own children, their parents are still available to give advice. Later in middle age, the person enters the ri stage. Their parents have become more like friends and are still available to give advice on those issues that may present difficulty.

Bonus Chapter
On Bunkai

Find this bonus chapter in the Hardcover edition.

About the Author

Kevin Dewayne Hughes is a martial artist, energy artist, fitness instructor, theologian, and scientist. He enjoys dabbling in all these fields and he plan to release titles in all these categories.

Martial arts: He is a long time instructor and student of Okinawan, Japanese, and Chinese arts.

Energy arts: He is a long time instructor and student of Yoga, Qi Gong, and Tai Chi.

Fitness: He use methods gained from martial and energy arts combined with modern methods.

Theology: He is an ordained minister of the Lord and delves deeply into studies of Christianity as well as understanding other religions.

Science: He is an electrical engineer and hydrogeologist by training. However, ha has taken opportunity to work in other fields. His geologic concentration has been on environmental issues on Earth and terraforming other planets.

Follow the author on TikTok at the following handles:

@kevkimhughes

@kdhughes_author

@stem.man

Follow the author on Facebook at the following link:

www.facebook.com/KevinKimberlyHughes

About the Tenkidokan

Tenkidokan is the name that Kevin Dewayne Hughes has chosen to call the training hall in which he teaches everything that he teaches. This includes more than just martial arts. It also includes energy arts, self-defense, fitness instruction, and anything else he wants to teach from his knowledge and skill pool.

There are four Chinese characters that make up the name Tenkidokan. Please note that the Japanese call Chinese characters by the term kanji. Also note that each kanji can have multiple readings called on and kun readings. Therefore, if you look up the readings of the kanji you will find that these characters can be read different ways. The four kanji are as follows:

Please take very careful notes of each character and it's meaning to fully understand how the name meaning is derived.

天 is ten and means heavens, sky, or imperial depending on context. We take the meaning of heaven in our compound of kanji.

氣 is ki and means energy, spirit, mind, air, atmosphere, breath, mood. We take the meaning of energy in our compound of kanji. Take note that in Japanese, this character is usually written as 気. The use of the classical Chinese character is two fold. The first and primary reason is because the Tenkidokan teaches things beyond Japanese martial arts and energy arts. The second reason is to show a difference between tenki in our usage verses the everyday usage of tenki in the Japanese language. In the Japanese language, 天気 (tenki) means weather. However, our usage of 天氣 (tenki) means heavenly energy.

道 is dou or do. Take note that this is said with a long o-sound but is usually written with a single o or an o with a bar over it to indicate a long o-sound. Do means way, journey, roadway, street, path, course, morals, or teachings. We use the kanji to mean way.

館 is kan and means building, mansion, large building, palace, a place or training hall. We use the kanji to mean a place or hall.

So the total reading of 天氣道館 (Tenkidokan) can be: A place to study the way of heavenly energy; training hall for the journey to heavenly energy; training hall to walk the path to heavenly energy; and many more renditions. We prefer the meaning to be: A place to study the way of heavenly energy.

The reason we use the term place instead of a building is because our studies are not restricted to inside a specific building. Our training hall is wherever we happen to be. It can be in our homes, in our yards, in a park, at gym, etc. The whole world and the whole universe is our training place and training hall.

A place to study the way of heavenly energy was chosen for several reasons:

1. The Tenkidokan teaches martial arts with a higher purpose beyond fight – we seek to

be upholders of the higher ground in all that
we do.

2. The Tenkidokan teaches energy arts,
which are things like Yoga and Qi Gong –
These lead to development of the mind,
body, and spirit.

3. The Tenkidokan teaches its members to
be morally upstanding members and
contributors to society.

4. The Tenkidokan teaches its members to
be defenders and protectors of others.

5. The Tenkidokan teaches virtues, such as
kindness, caring, and charity to others.

6. The Tenkidokan teaches to continually
grow and refine to higher and higher levels of
perfection.

7. The Tenkidokan teaches to continually
become more and more enlightened.

Members of the Tenkidokan are expected to
uphold the meaning of the name and the
reasons why the name was chosen.

The Weather

Even if someone insists that tenki must mean weather, then that is an ok meaning too. Weather, after all, can be calming and peaceful to the ultimate raging violence. When weather is violent, it always wins.

Weather also incorporates all the elements. In the common five elements system of China where metal, earth, wood, fire, and water are the elements, weather incorporates them all. Fire is seen in lightening, especially when lightening catches things on fire. The rains that weather can deliver can cause life to grow and flourish or it can wipe life out in torrential down pours and flooding. Tornadoes, hurricanes, and straight wind burst can pick up and hurl metal, rocks, and wood and this incorporates the elements of earth and wood. Wood represents life, and as stated above, life needs the weather to thrive. Earth is further seen in weather in the form of sand storms and dust devils.

In the Japanese five elements system of fire, earth, water, sky, and void, weather influences all five. Fire is moved and fed by moving air, the winds, but fire is quenched by water. The moving waters and wind blown particles shape the earth. The sky is the domain of weather and the weather in the void dwarfs anything seen on the Earth. The celestial weather of the stars is an awesome phenomenon that creates beauty in both creation and destruction.

Weather can bring comfortable warmth and cool that relaxes and calms. Weather can also bring about deathly heat and cold. There is nothing in the material realm not affected by weather. Even an objected in space is deteriorated by the bombardment of particles moving on the celestial winds.

Tenkidokan translated at the way of weather or as the way of heavenly energy both completely embody the philosophy of Kevin Dewayne Hughes.

A bonus thought on the subject. Weathering also means to endure and enduring hardships and trials is a good skill to have. It is thus another trait the Tenkidokan teaches to its students.

Follow the Tenkidokan on TikTok at the following handles:
@Tenkidokan
@Tenkidokan_Fitness
@Tenkidokan_Iron_Body
@Tenkidokan_Weapons

Follow the Tenkidokan on Facebook at the link:

 www.facebook.com/Tenkidokan

Follow the Tenkidokan on Instagram at the handle:

@Tenkidokan

Follow the Tenkidokan on Twitter at the handle:

@Tenkidokan

Follow the Tenkidokan on Youtube at the following link:

www.youtube.com/Tenkidokan